Thank You
for purchasing this journal.
St. Simon's Learning Institute

A Letter to Parents

Dear Parents,

As you well know, the year 2020 through to 2021 has been a sequence of challenging events for our nation, Barbados and the world at large. Our children have had to deal with changing routines, lockdowns and quarantines. Not to mention online schooling, mask-wearing and most recently dealing with the severe ashfall from the eruptions of La Soufriére volcano of St Vincent, a neighbouring island.

These events have made our children (students) anxious, fearful and uncertain. Studies have shown that creating awareness of mindfulness in children helps develop healthy mental functions in children, allowing them to be less anxious about the natural occasions of uncertainty in their lives.

Children's very own expression of gratitude for the things and people they have around them creates positivity and happy feelings thus allowing them to have a more positive outlook about the current challenges.

This journal seeks to do just that by creating feelings of joy and happiness within each user. Five minutes each day is enough to give every child who uses this journal enough pleasant thoughts to feel more peace and less anxiety during the day and beyond.

Daily use of the journal is encouraged for maximum results.

Thank you and continue to stay safe.


Lisa A. Badenock

Principal & Founder

St. Simon's Learning Institute

Date: ______________________________

# I am thankful for.....

**Today I feel**

**This person made me feel happy today**
______________________________

Date: ___________________________________

Draw a picture or write in each heart.

# I am thankful for.....

# Inspirational Quotes

**Date:** _______________________________

# I am thankful for.....

1. _______________________________

2. _______________________________

3. _______________________________

4. _______________________________

**Today I feel** 

Draw or write in the heart.
The best of part my day was .....

Date: _______________________

# I am grateful for.....

## Today I feel

## These things make me happy....

# Inspirational Quotes

Date: _______________________________

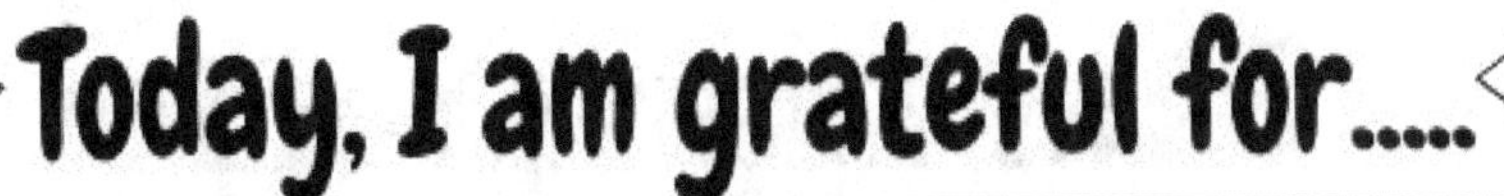

Today I feel

This person made me feel happy today:

_______________________________

Date: _______________________

# I am thankful for.....

## Today I feel

## My favourite things are:

# Inspirational
# Quotes

**Date:** ______________________

# I am grateful for.....

1. ______________________

2. ______________________

3. ______________________

4. ______________________

Today I feel 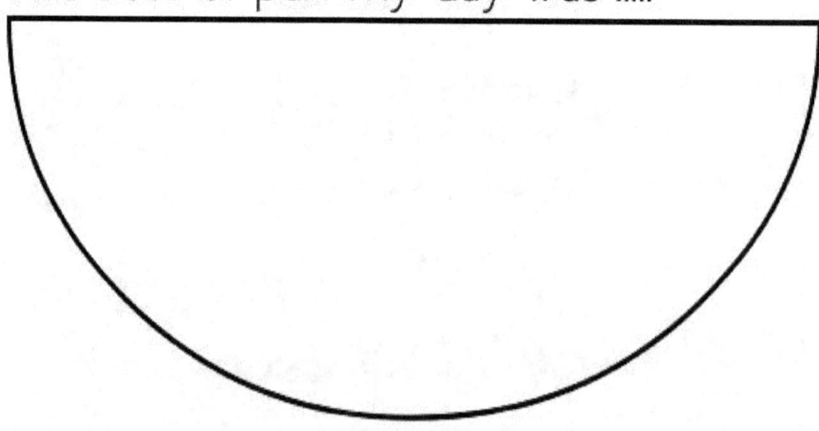

Draw or write in the semi-circle.

The best of part my day was .....

# I AM THANKFUL FOR...

Colour the words

This person added to my joy today:

# Inspirational
# Quotes

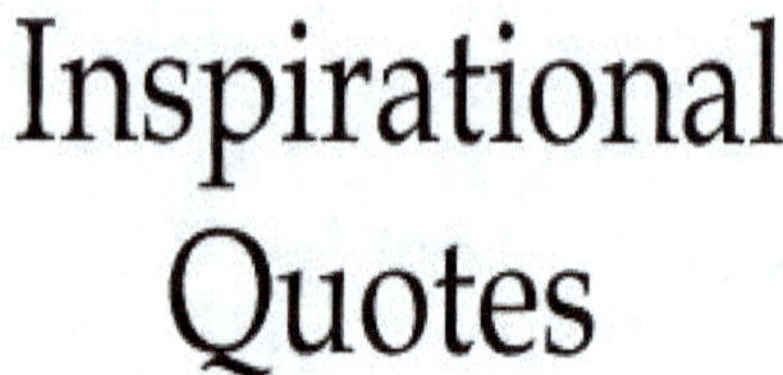

"The more grateful I am, the
more beauty I see! "

Mary Davis

Date: ___________________________________

Draw a picture or write in each book.

# I am thankful for.....

Today I feel

I talked to this person today and it felt great!

**Date:** ___________________________

# I AM BLESSED WITH ...

## Colour the words

good health

a loving family

kind friends

a comfortable home

getting a good education

daily food

good teachers

a happy life

Today I feel 

I love me and I am .....

# Inspirational Quotes

Date: ___________________________



Write a thank you note to someone.

Today I feel

My best friend makes me smile, My best friend's name is .....

Date: _______________________________

**Today I feel**

What nice words did you say today?

_______________________________

_______________________________

Date: ______________________________



Draw a picture of the people you love.

Today I feel

Who are you thankful for?

______________________________

______________________________

**Date:** _______________________________

# My Teachers Love Me Too

Draw a picture of you and your teacher.

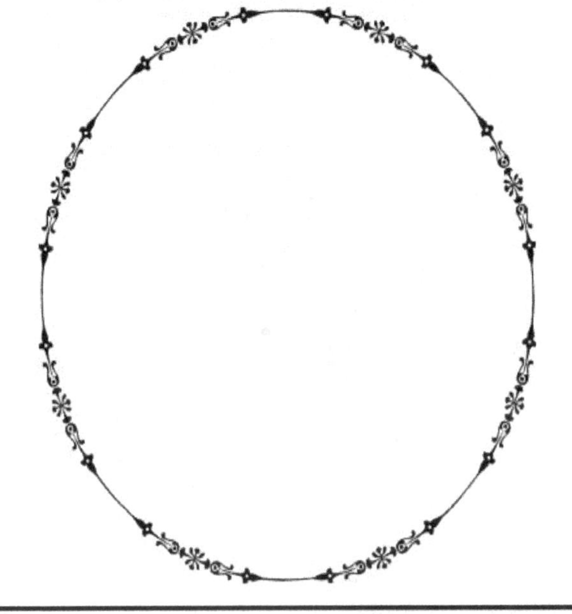

Today I feel

I am thankful for my teacher because.....

_______________________________

_______________________________

# Inspirational Quotes

Date: _______________________________



Draw or write what you can do in the box.

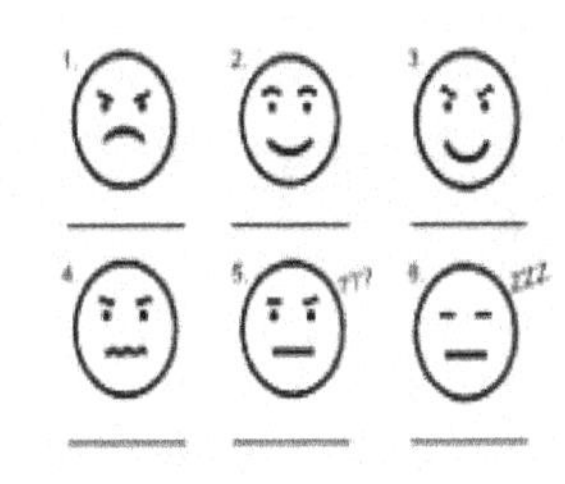

Today I feel

I like to ........

_______________________________

_______________________________

Date: ___________________________________

**Today I feel**

# I am thankful for my family because...

_______________________________________

TODAY
I AM
*thankful*

Date: _______________________________

**Draw or paste photos of what makes you feel good.**

Today I feel

Date: _______________________________

**Draw or paste photos of what makes you feel good.**

# My Thank You Notes

# My Thank You Notes

# My Thank You Notes

# My Thank You Notes

Date: ___________________________________

# Today I feel

## This person made me feel happy today

___________________________________

Date: _______________________

Draw a picture or write in each heart.

# I am thankful for.....

Today I feel

I helped this person today:

_______________________

Love is the greatest gift of all

**Date:** _______________________________

# I am thankful for.....

1. _______________________________

2. _______________________________

3. _______________________________

4. _______________________________

## Today I feel

Draw or write in the heart.
The best of part my day was .....

Date: ___________________________

# I am grateful for.....

# Today I feel

# These things make me happy....

# Sing, Laugh and Dance

Date: ______________________________

# I am thankful for.....

# Today I feel

# My favourite things are:

NEVER
give up

**Date:** _______________________________

# I am grateful for.....

1. _______________________________

2. _______________________________

3. _______________________________

4. _______________________________

Today I feel 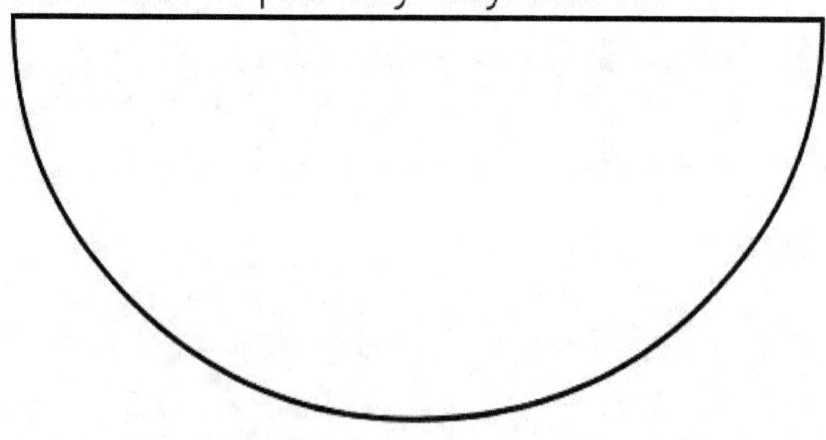

Draw or write in the semi-circle.

The best of part my day was .....

# I AM THANKFUL FOR...

## Colour the words

This person added to my joy today:

Start each day with a grateful heart!

Date: _______________________________________

Draw a picture or write in each book.

# I am thankful for.....

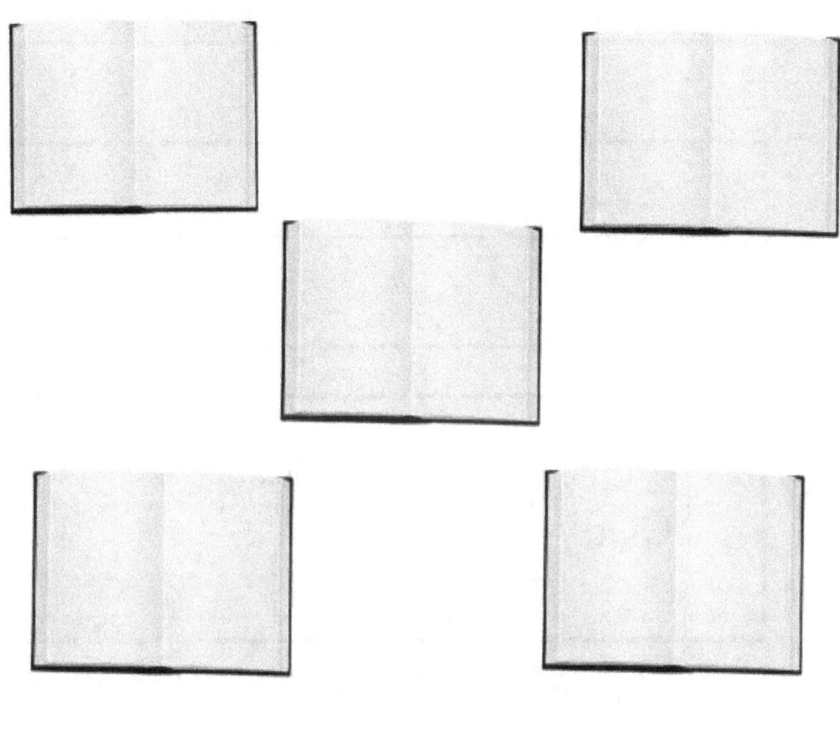

Today I feel

I talked to this person today and it felt great!

**Date:** _______________________

# I am grateful for.....

1. _______________________

2. _______________________

3. _______________________

4. _______________________

Today I feel 

Draw or write in the semi-circle.

The best of part my day was .....

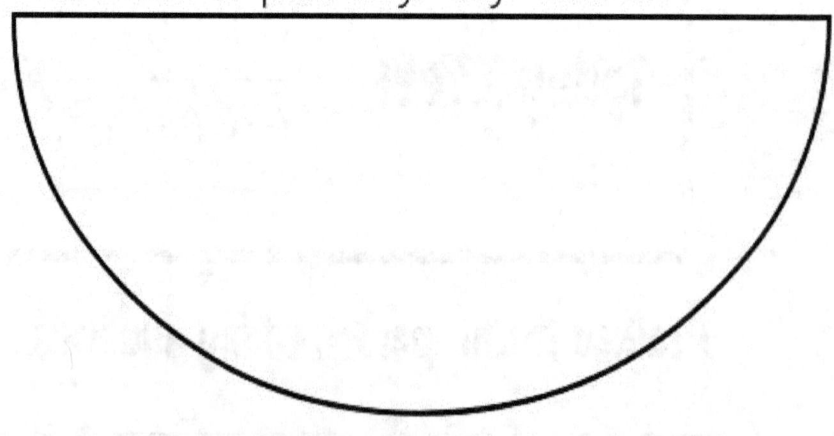

There is
ALWAYS
something to be
grateful
for!

# Thank you!

Write a thank you note to someone.

Today I feel

My best friend makes me smile, My best friend's name is …..

Date: ______________________________

Today I feel

## What nice words did you say today?

______________________________

______________________________

ENJOY
EVERY
MOMENT

Date: _______________________________



Draw a picture of the people you love.

Today I feel

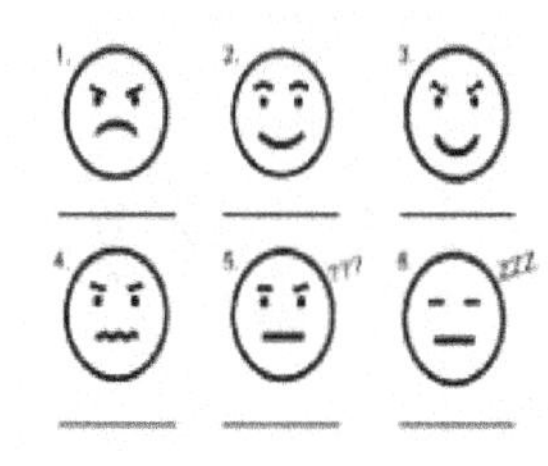

Who are you thankful for?

_______________________________

_______________________________

Date: ___________________________________



Draw a picture of you and your teacher.

Today I feel 

I am thankful for my teacher because.....

_______________________________________

_______________________________________

# A kind friend

Is the right friend.

Date: _______________________________



Draw or write what you can do in the box.

I can ......

Today I feel

I like to ........

_______________________________

_______________________________

Date: ______________________________

**Today I feel**

I am thankful for my family because...

______________________________

Every day may not be good, but there is GOOD in every day.

Date: _______________________

## Draw or paste photos of what makes you feel good.

Today I feel

Date: _______________________

**Draw or paste photos of what makes you feel good.**

**Today I feel**

BElieve in
YOUr Self

# List of Ways I will Show Love Today

# List of Ways I will Show Love Today

# List of Ways I will Show Love Today

FIND THE GOOD
AND BE HAPPY IN
IT

Date: _______________________________

**Draw or paste photos of what makes you feel good.**

**Today I feel**

# Draw or paste photos of what makes you feel good.

## Today I feel

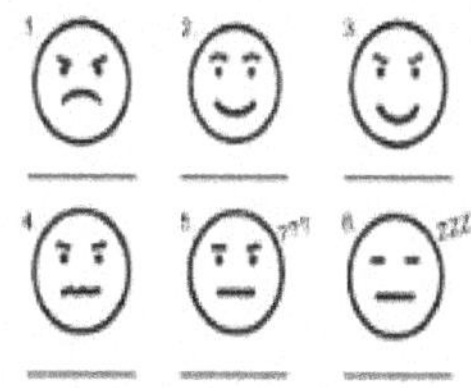

Dream Big
Say Please and Thank You
BE GRATEFUL

Date: _______________________________

# I am grateful for.....

## Today I feel

## These things make me happy....

**Date:** ______________________________

## I am grateful for.....

1. ______________________________

2. ______________________________

3. ______________________________

4. ______________________________

Today I feel

Draw or write in the semi-circle.

The best of part my day was .....

# My Thank You Notes

# My Thank You Notes

Be
Thankful

# List of Ways I will Show Love Today

# List of Ways I will Show Love Today

Thank You!